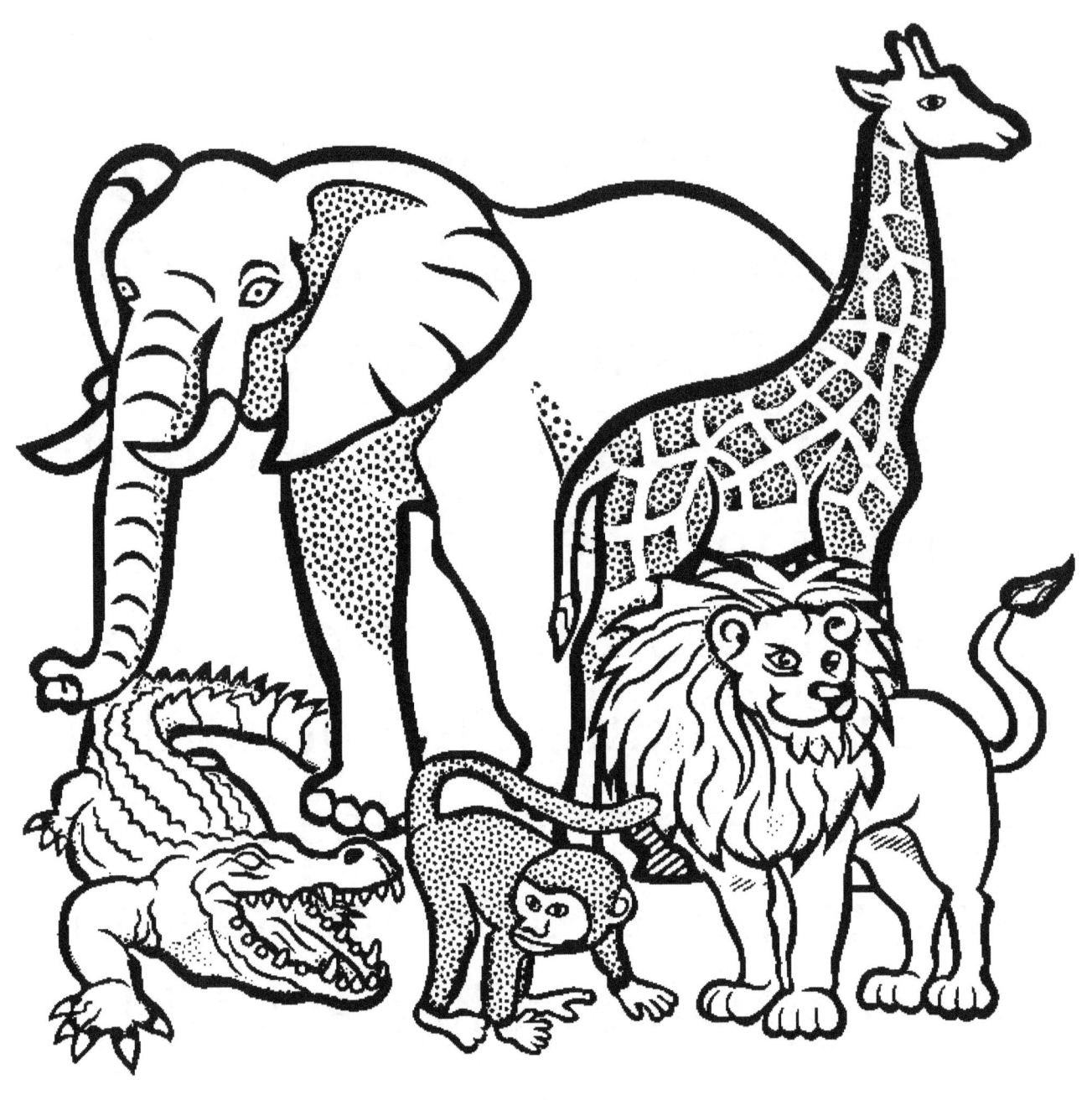

Are you ready ?

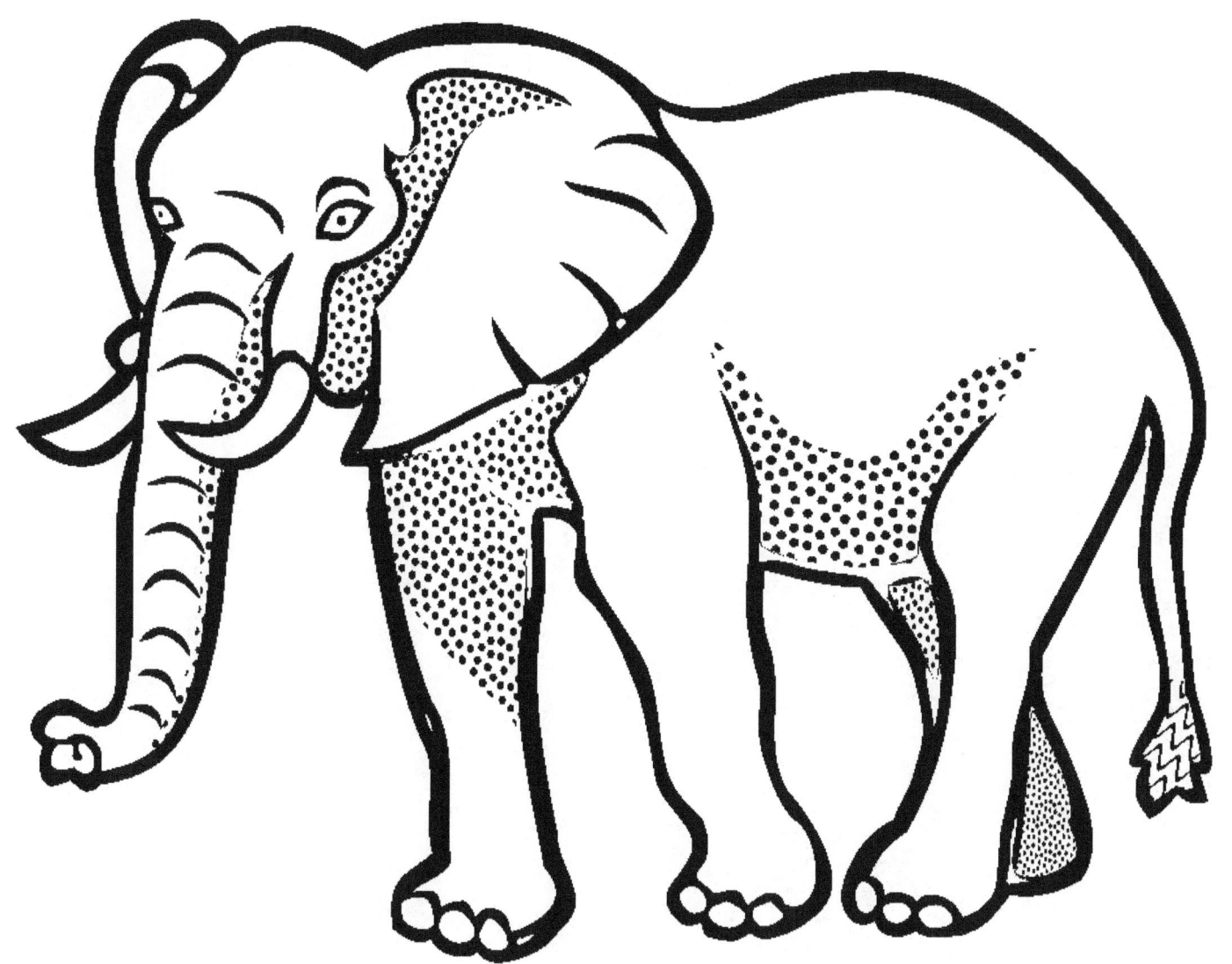

# ELEPHANT

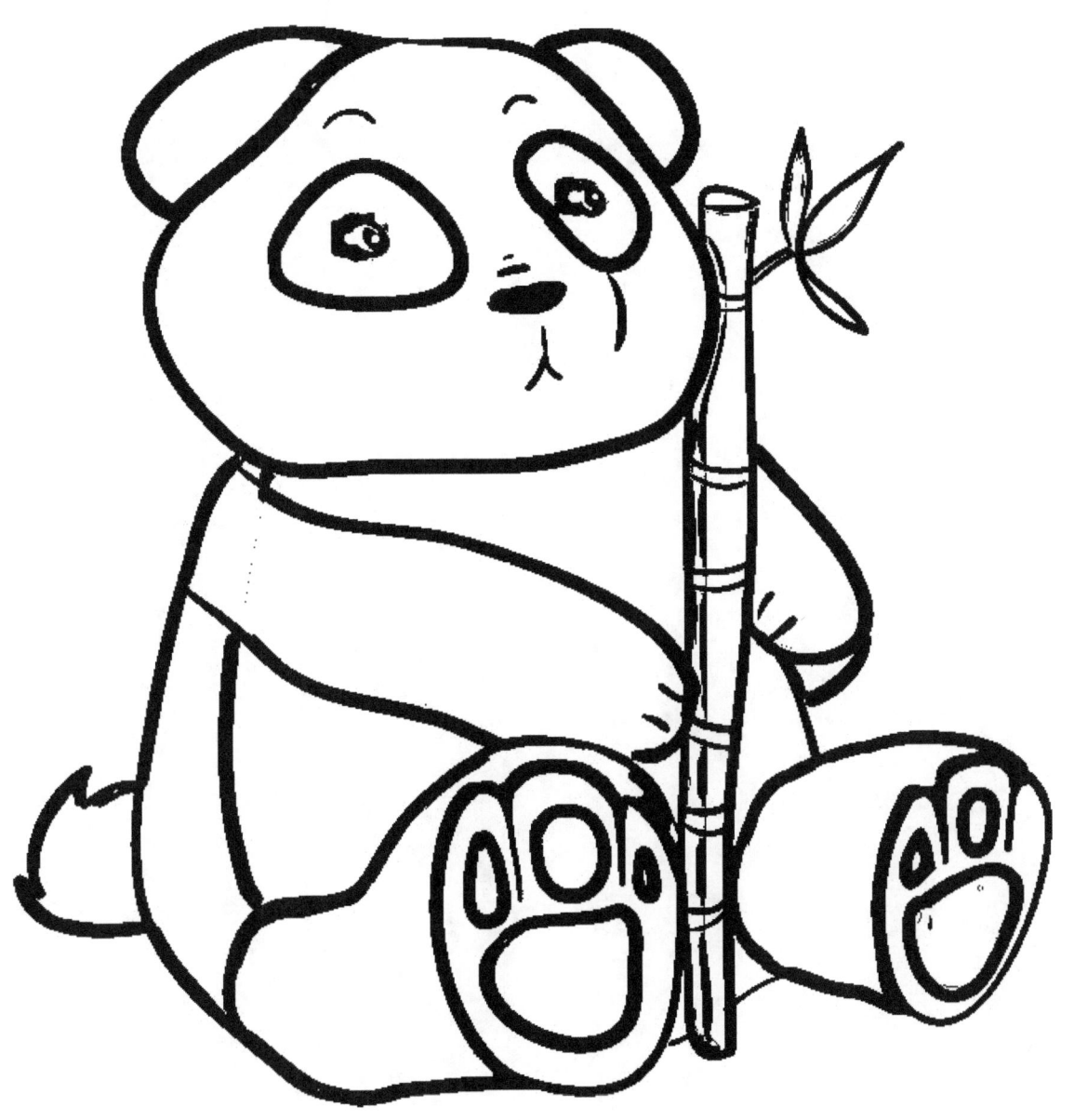

# PANDA

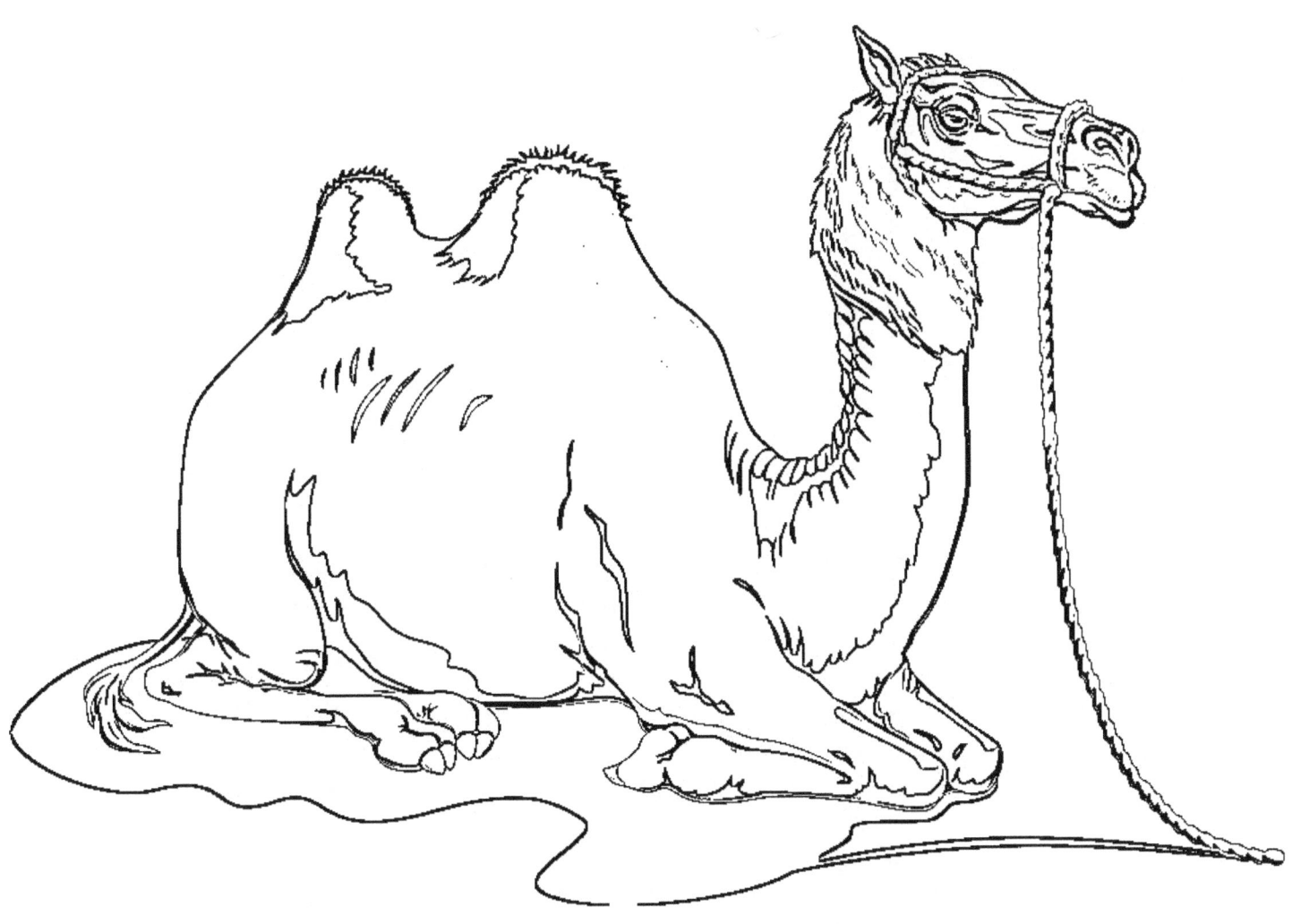

# CAMEL

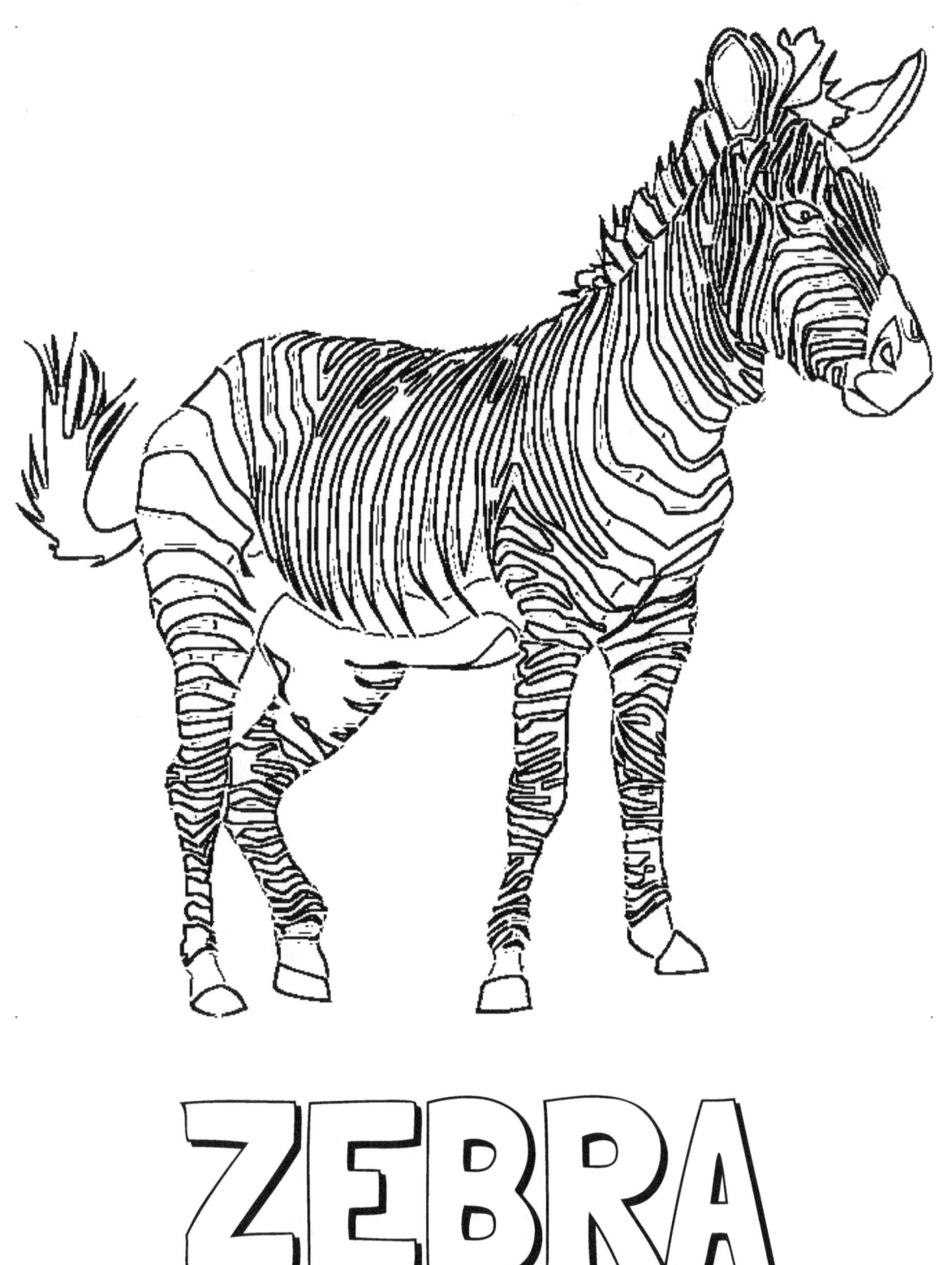

ZEBRA

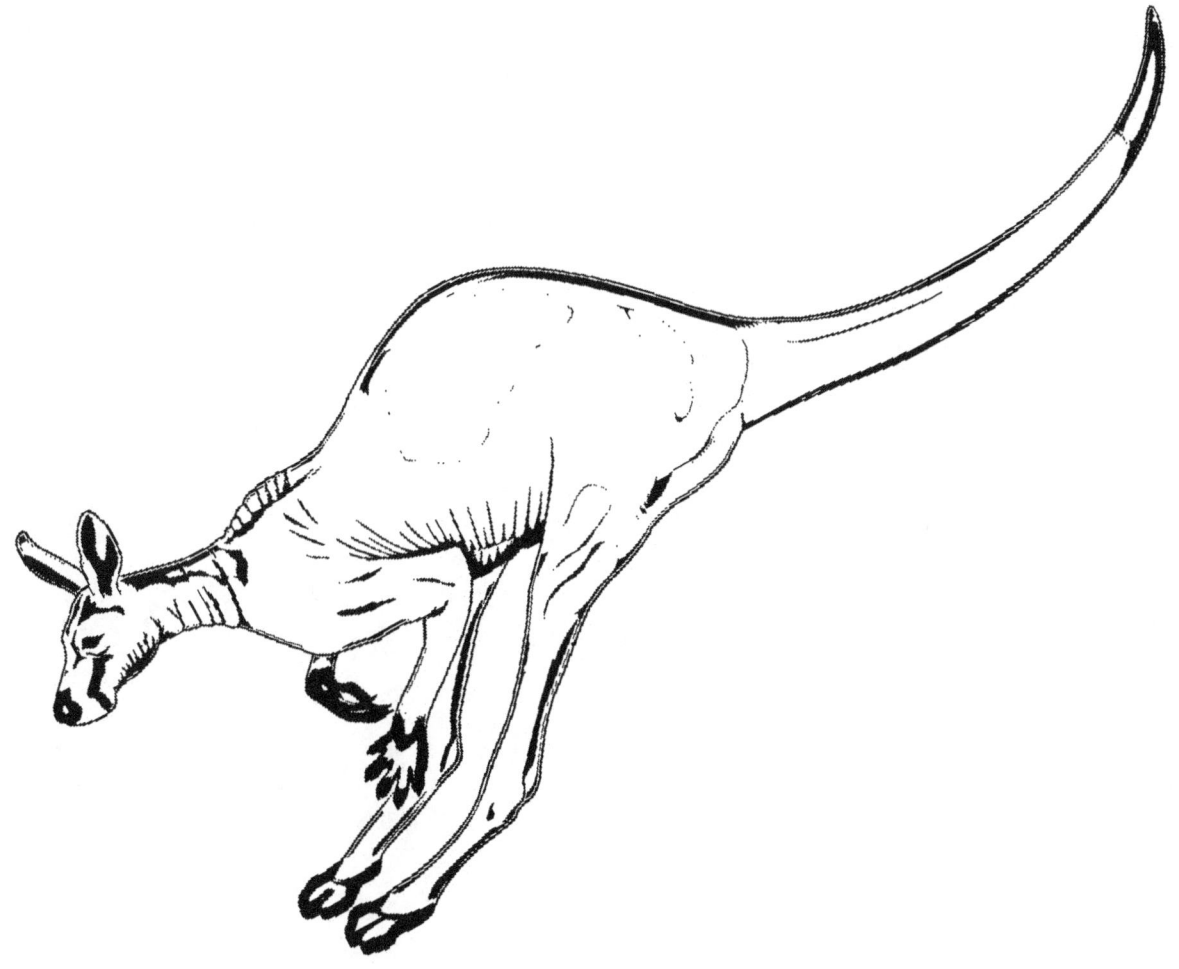

# KANGAROO

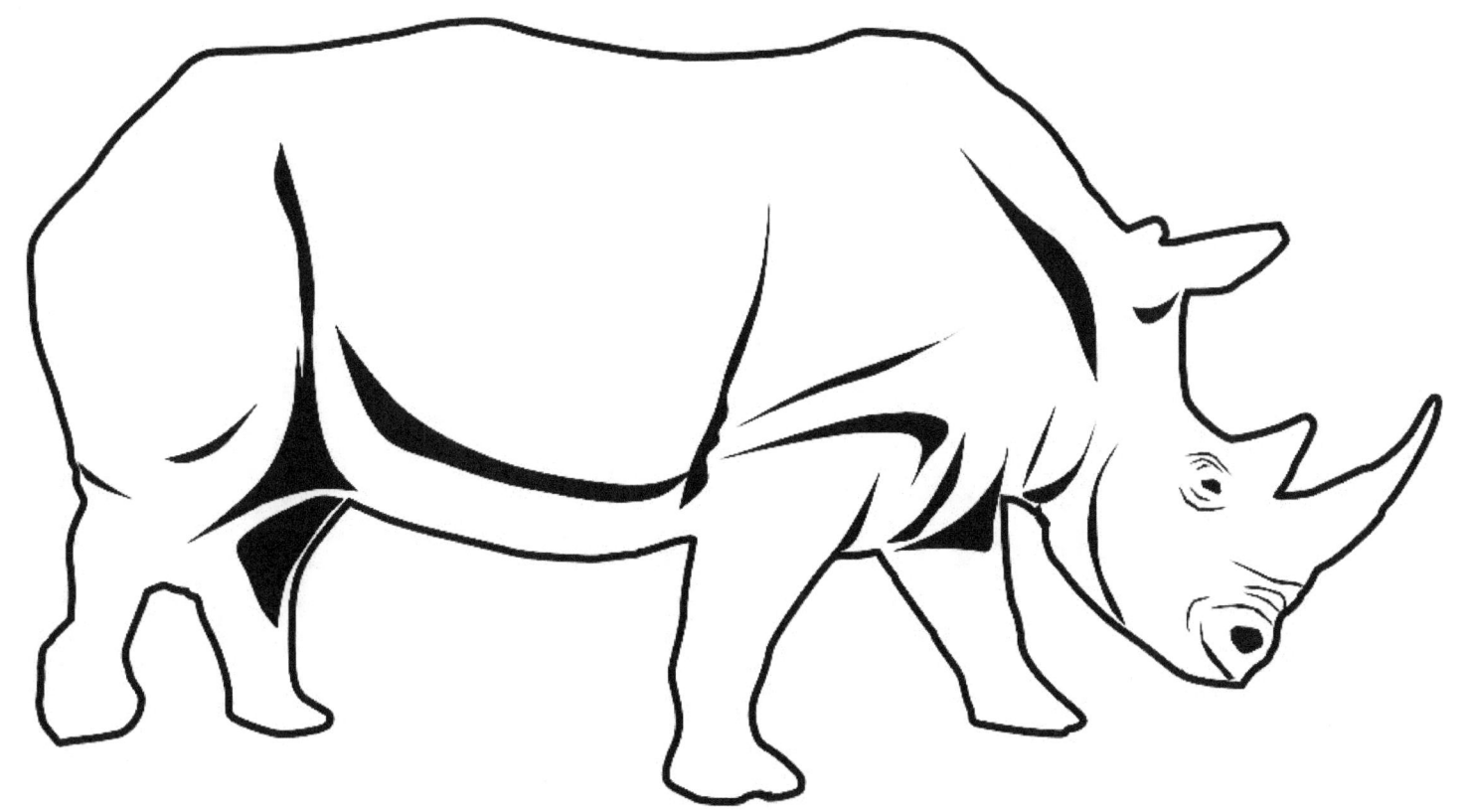

RHINO

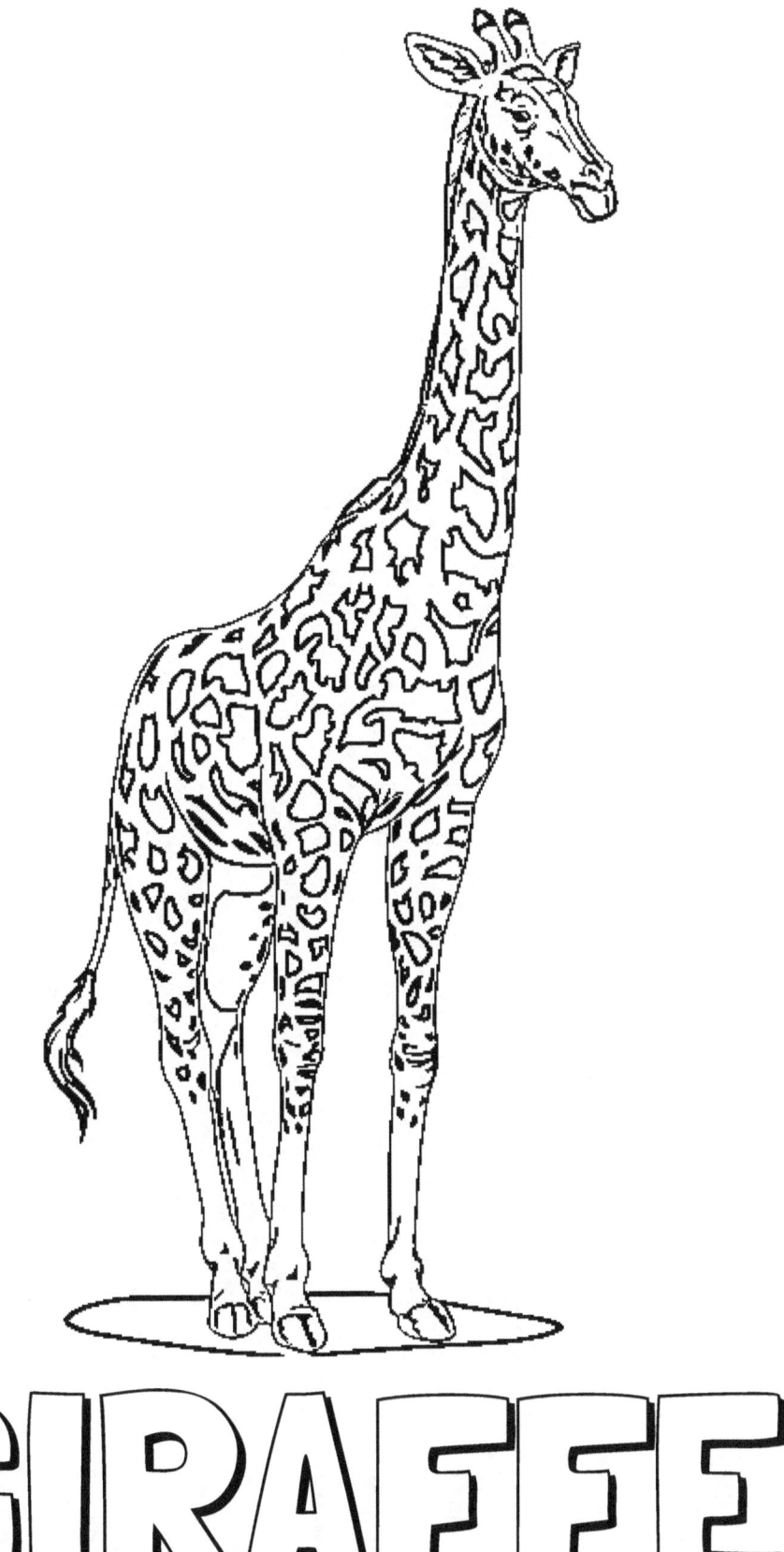

# GIRAFFE

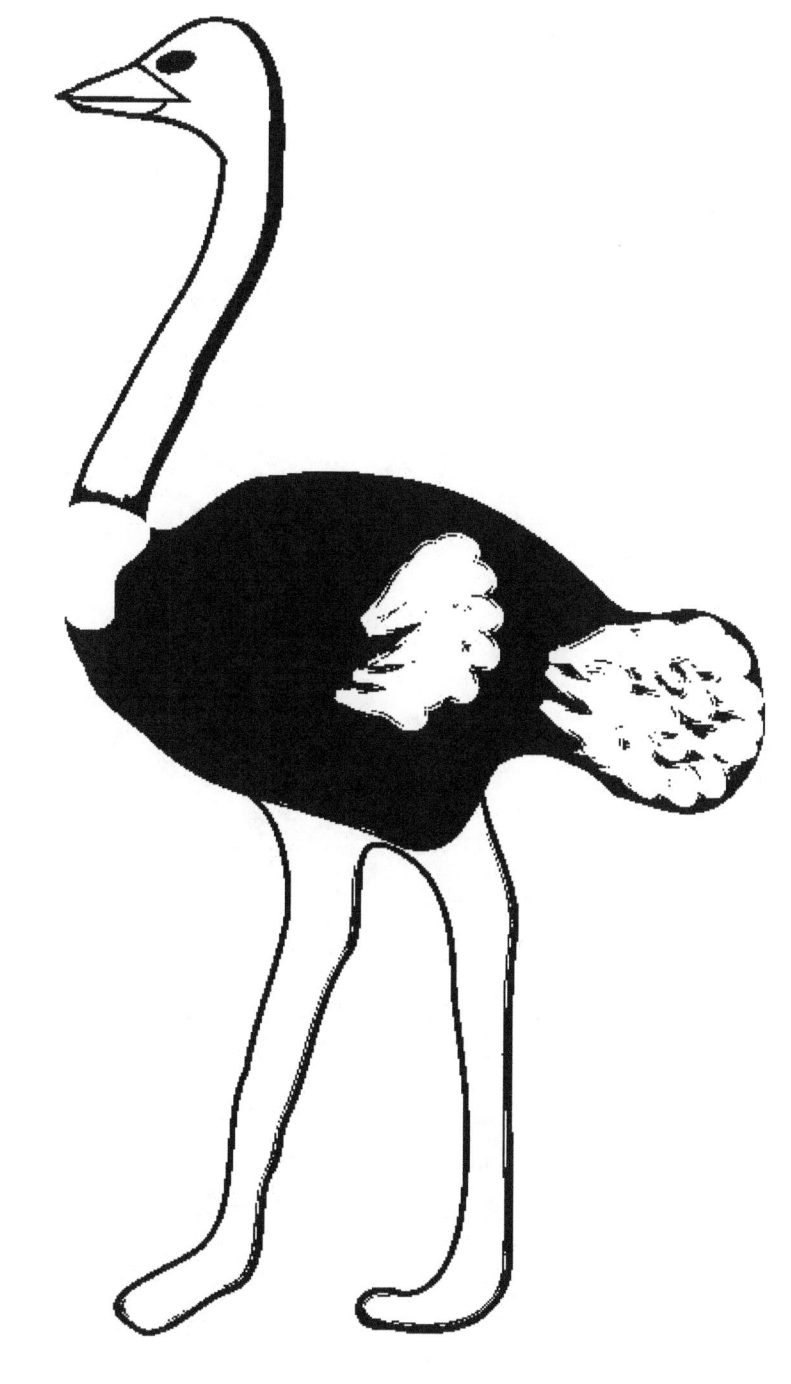

# OSTRICH

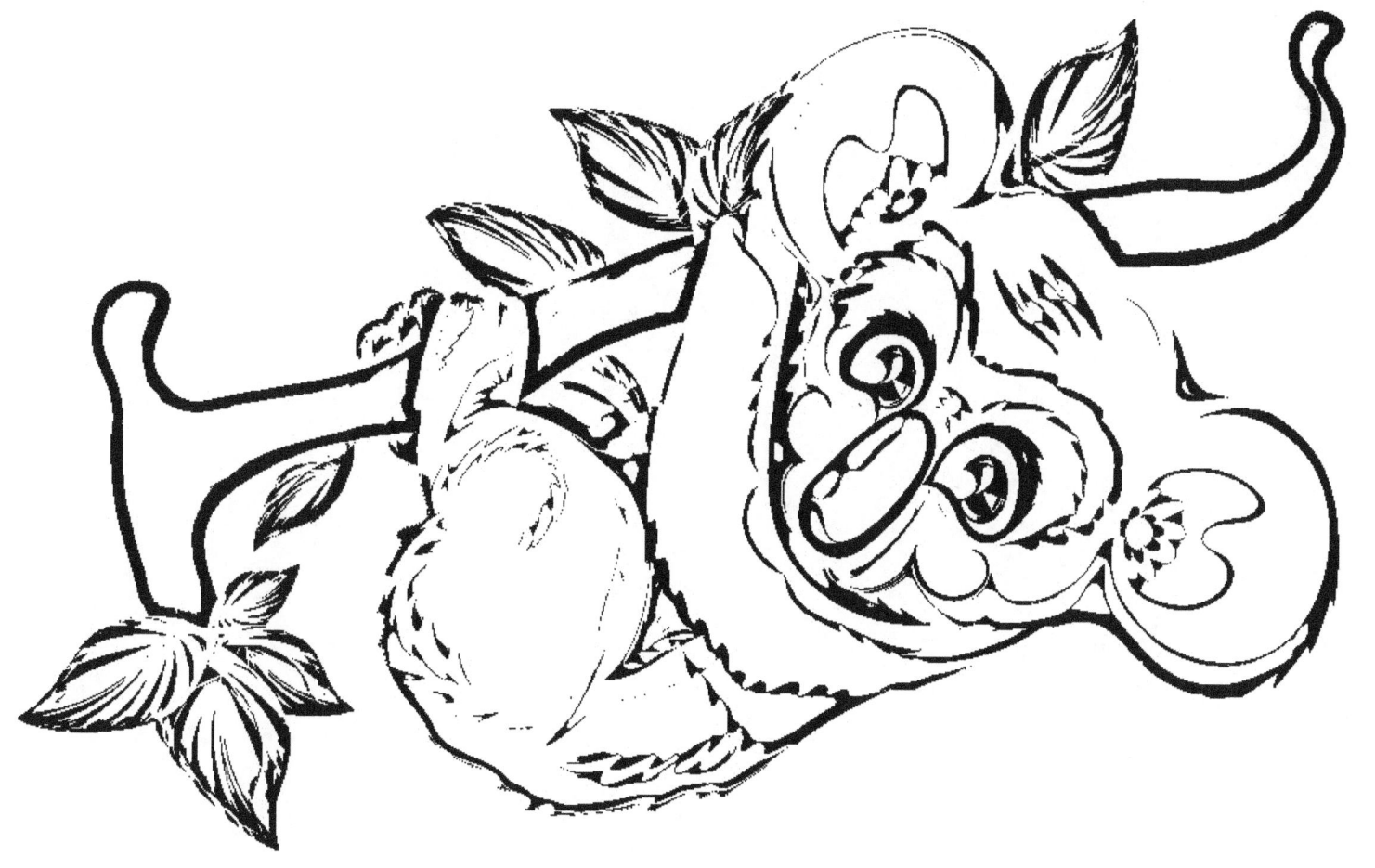

# KOALA

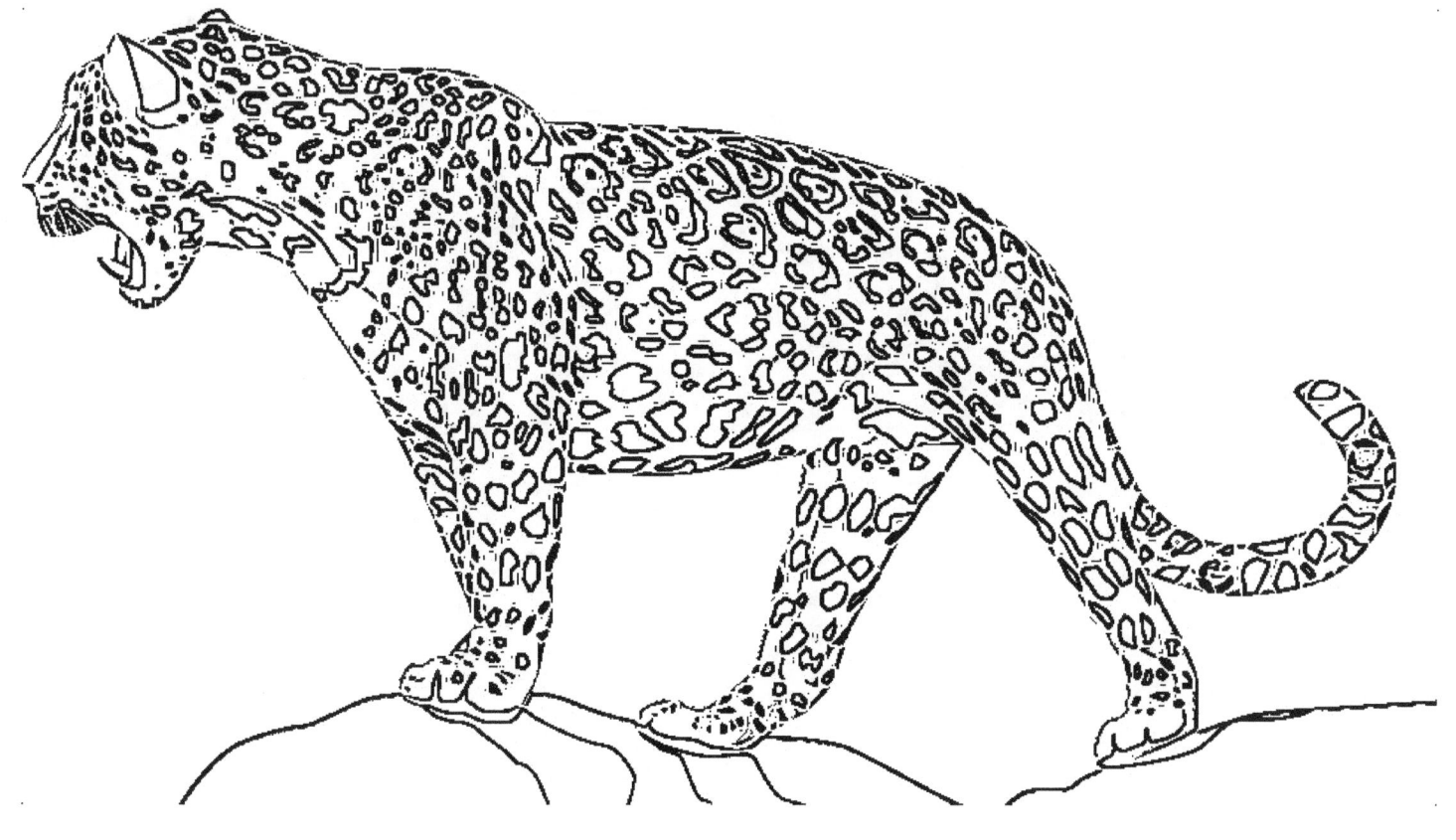

# LEOPARD

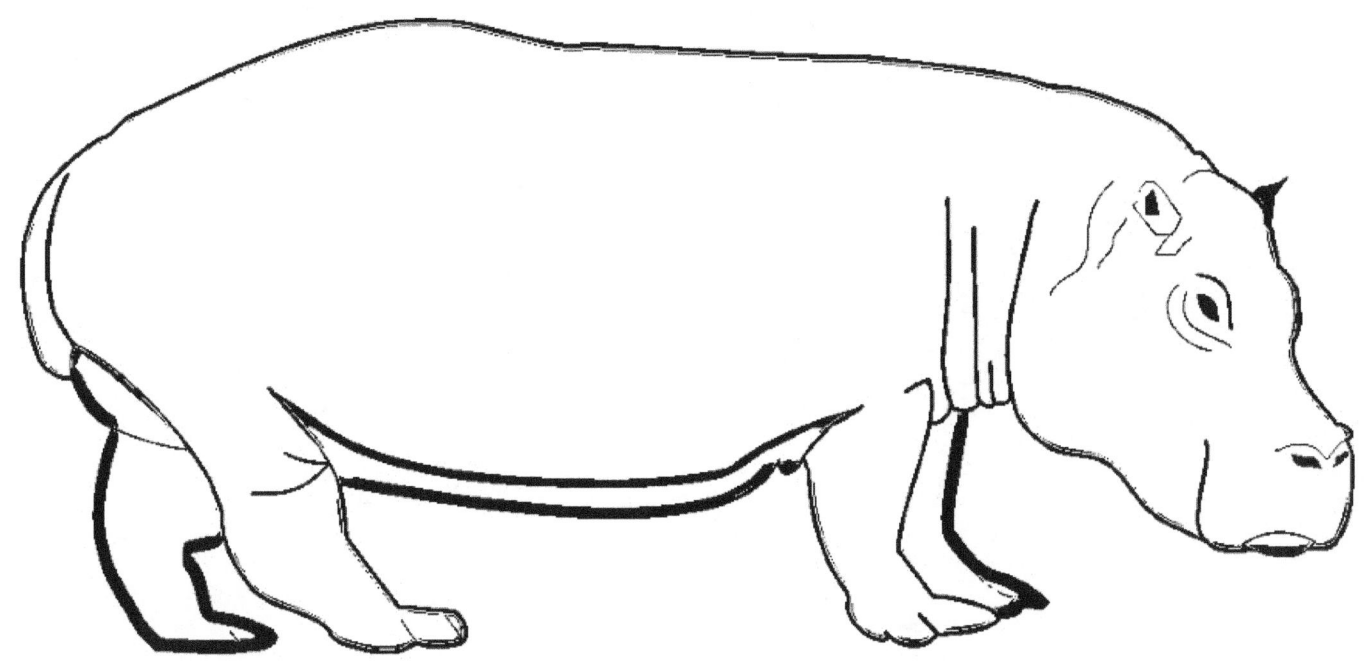

# HIPPOPOTAMUS

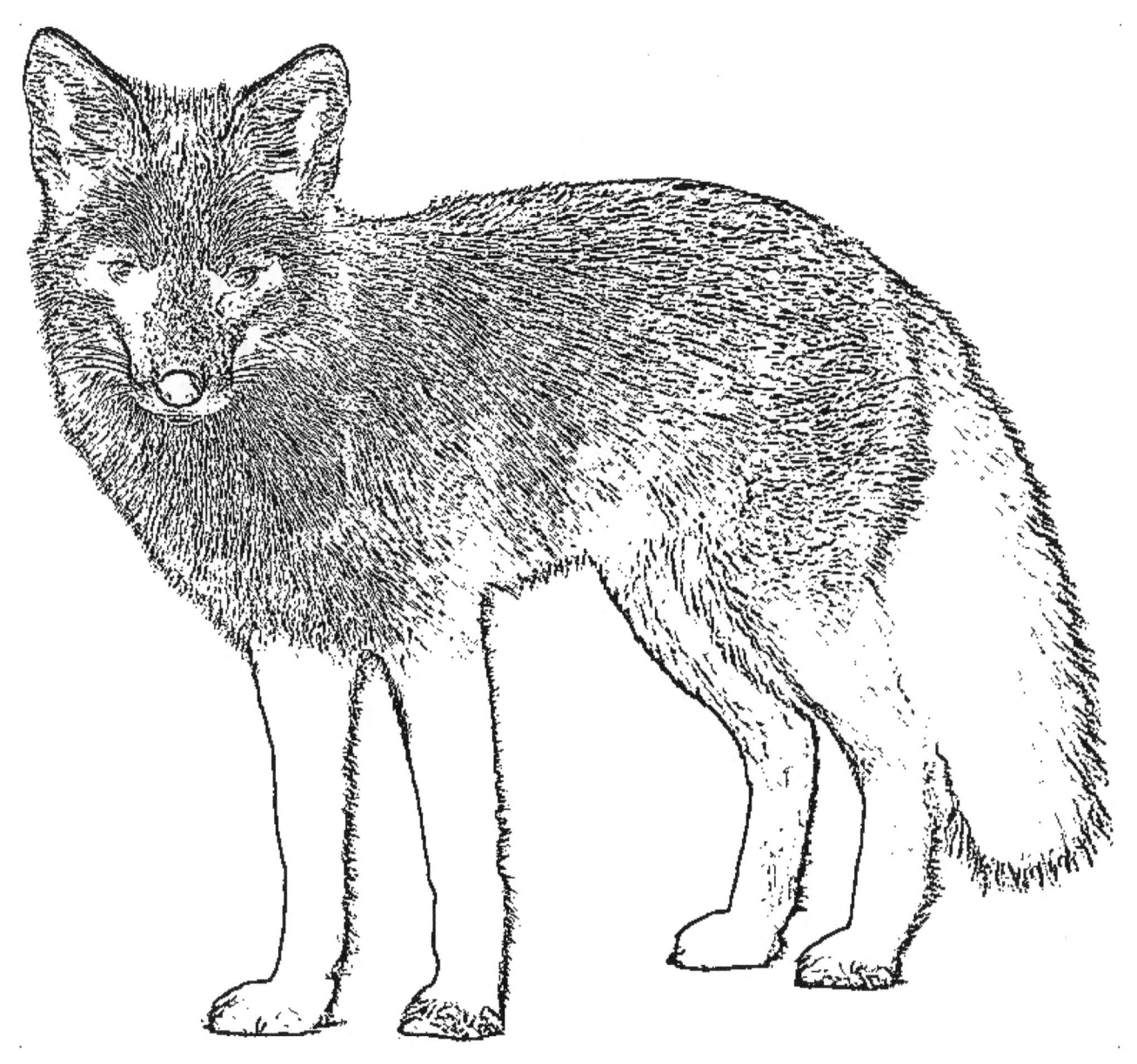

# FOX

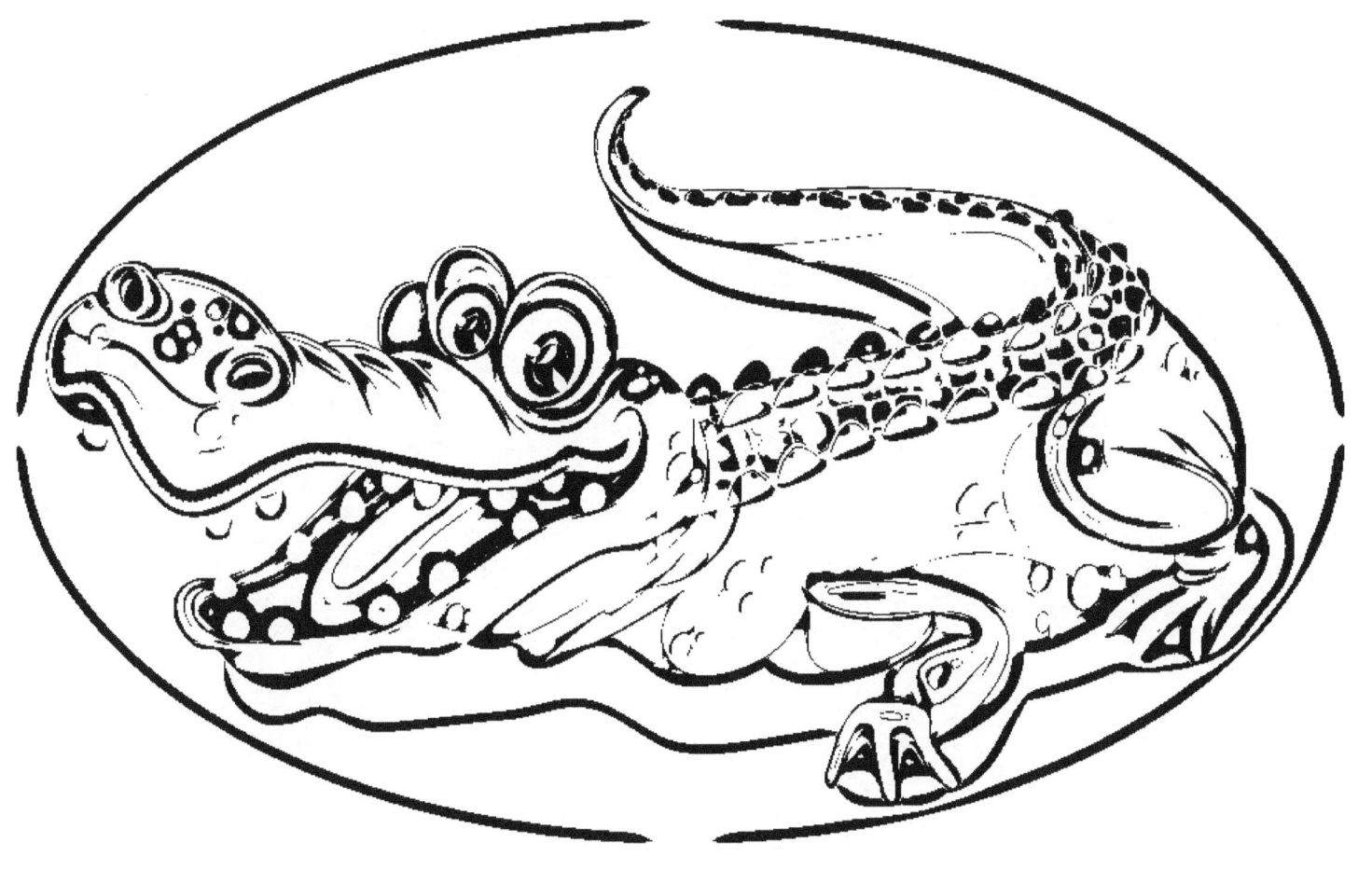

# CROCODILE

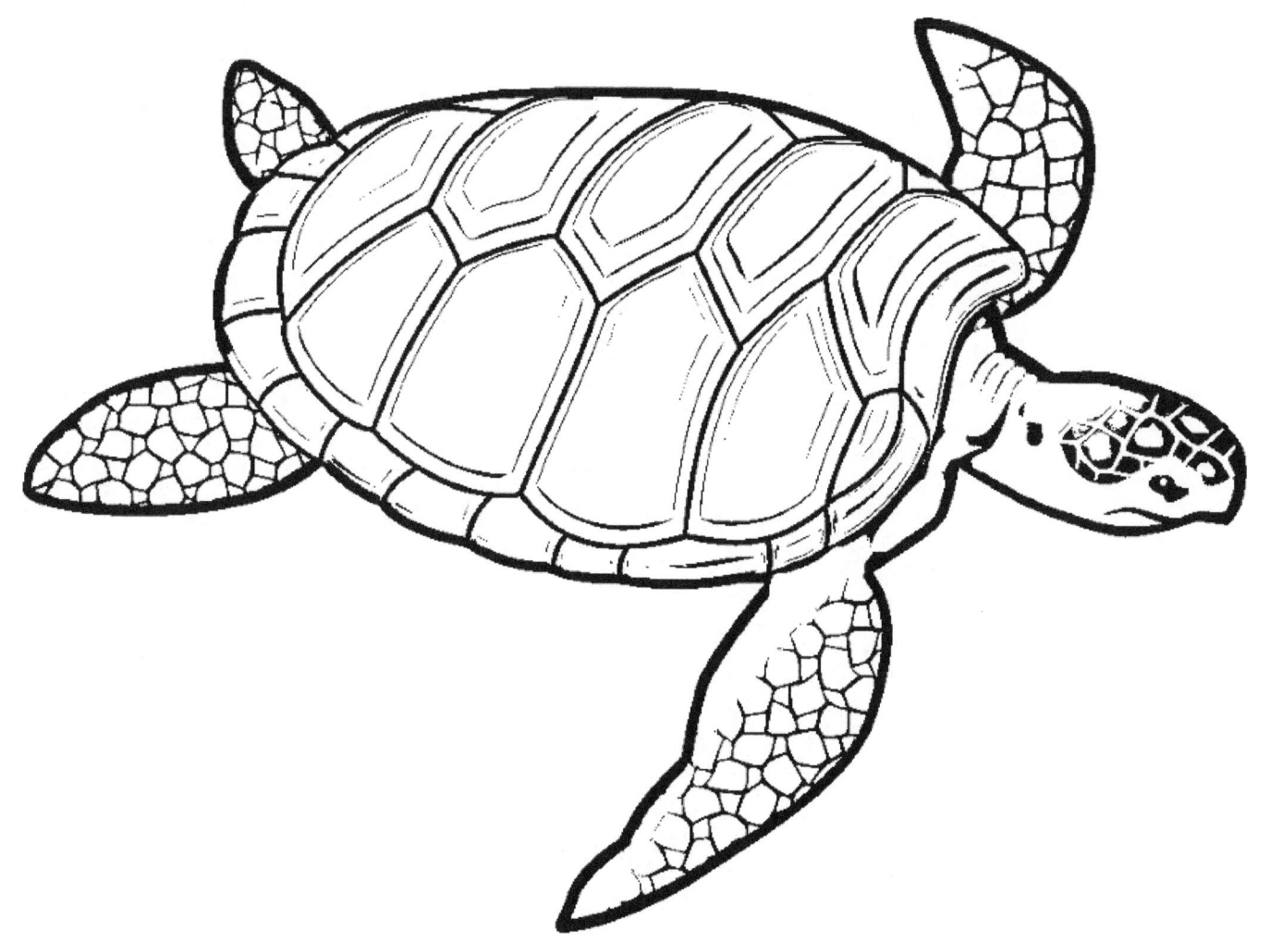

# SEA TURTLE

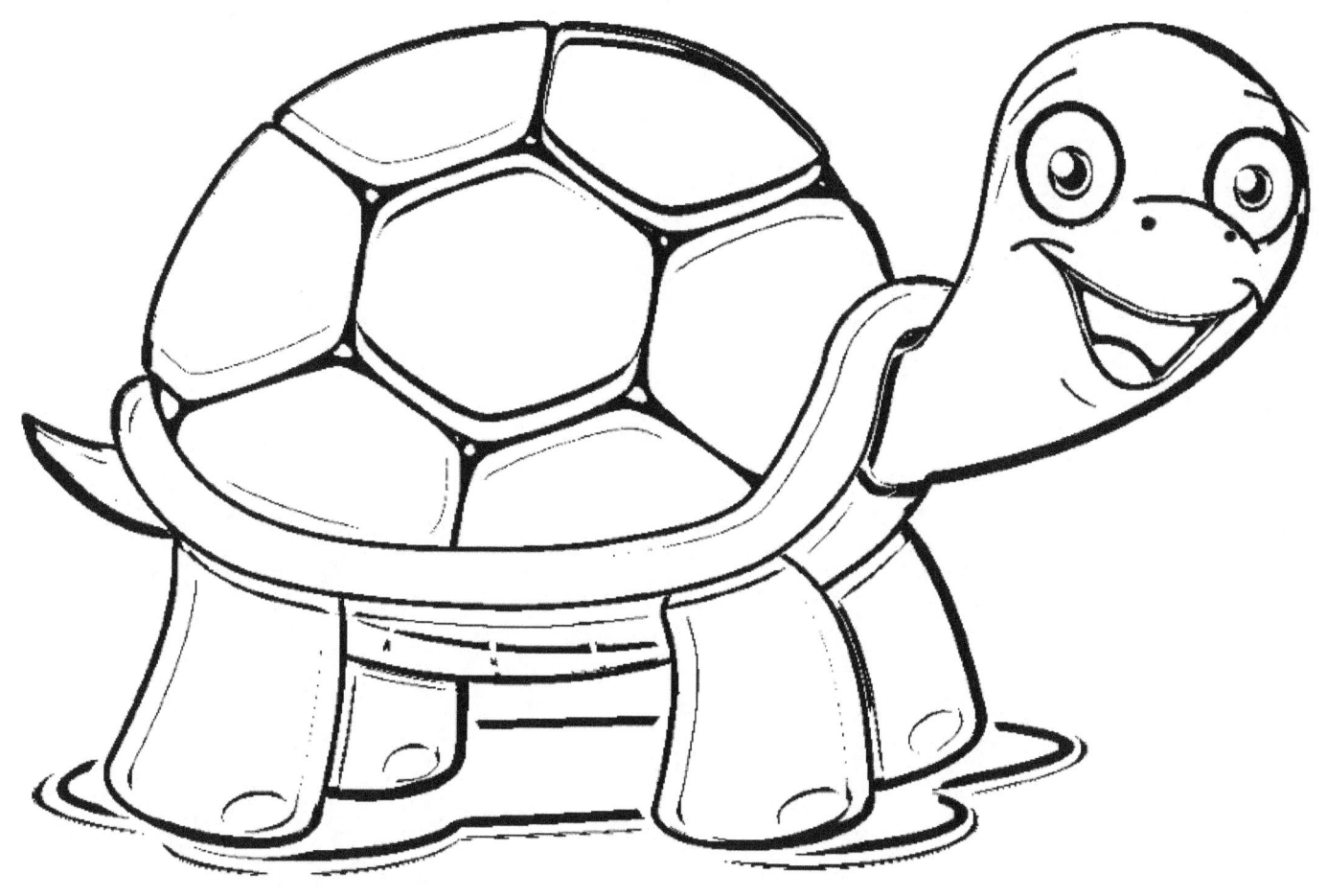

# TURTLE

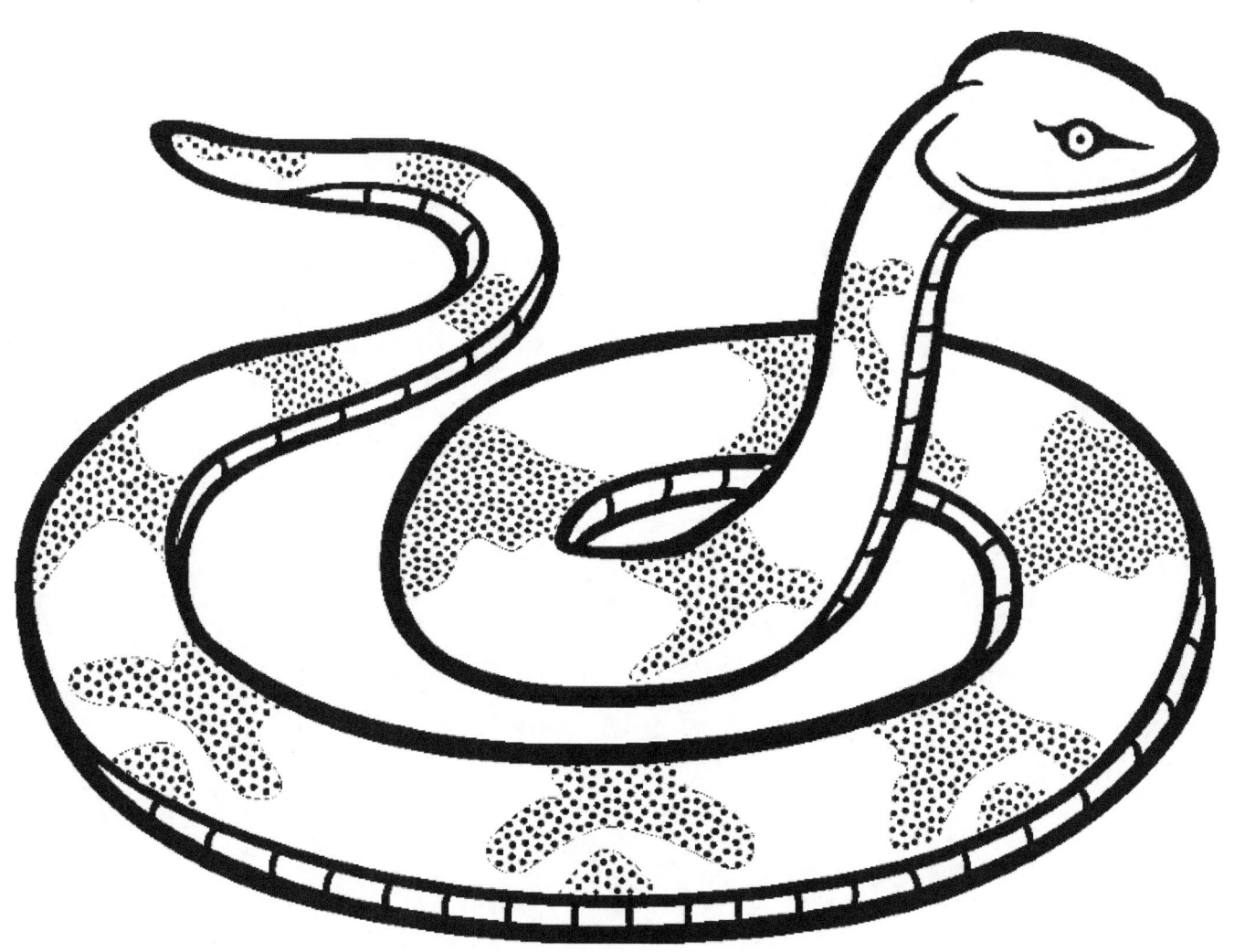

# SNAKE

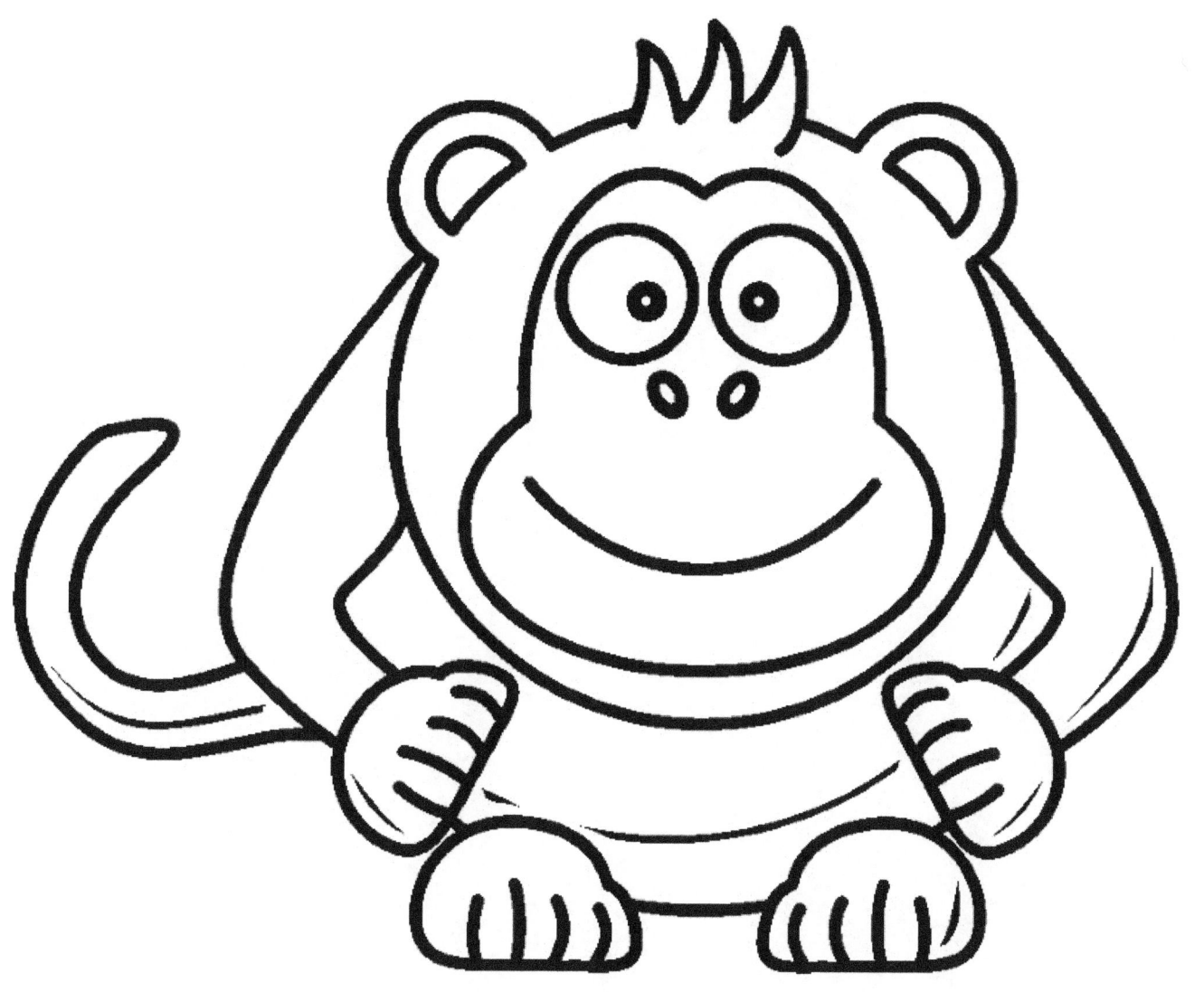

# MONKEY

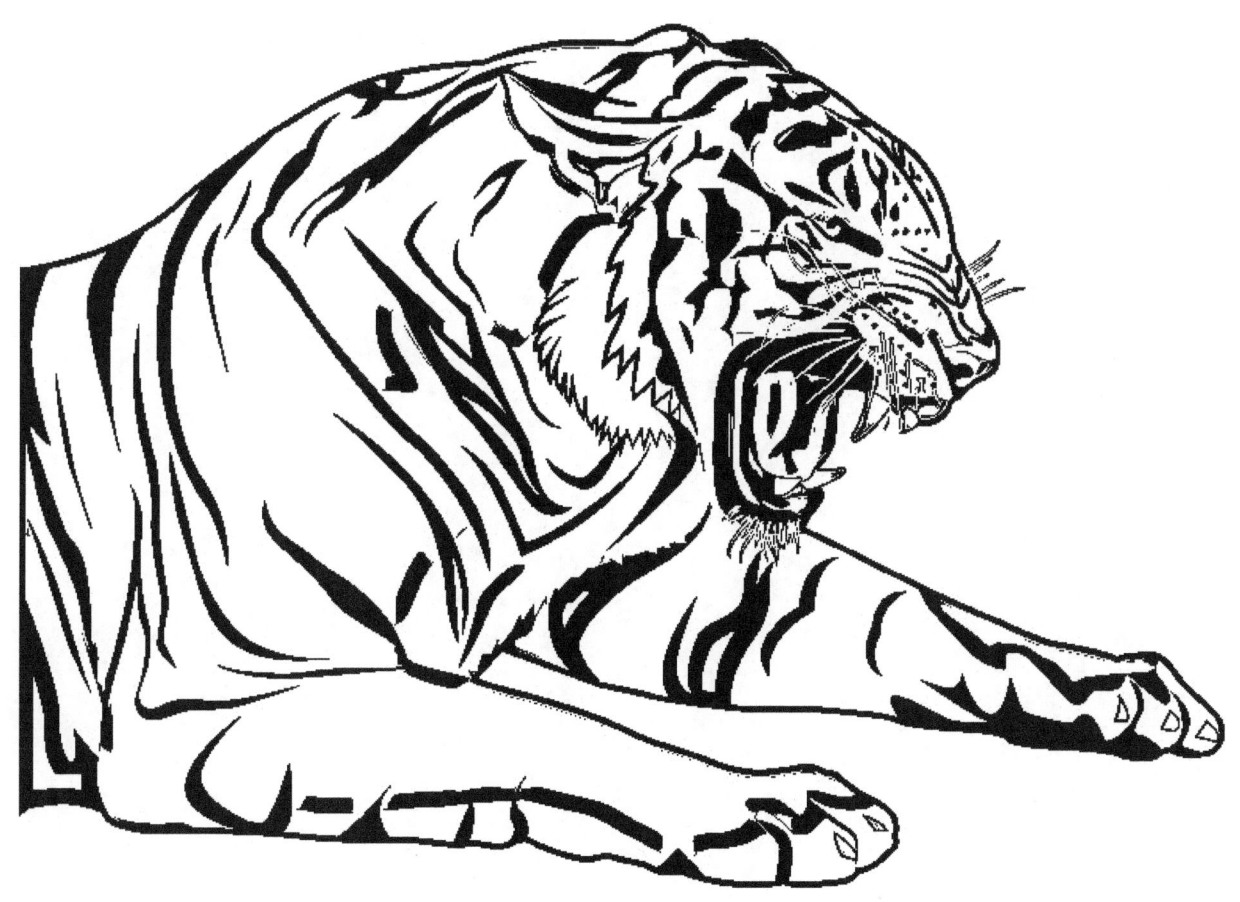

# TIGER

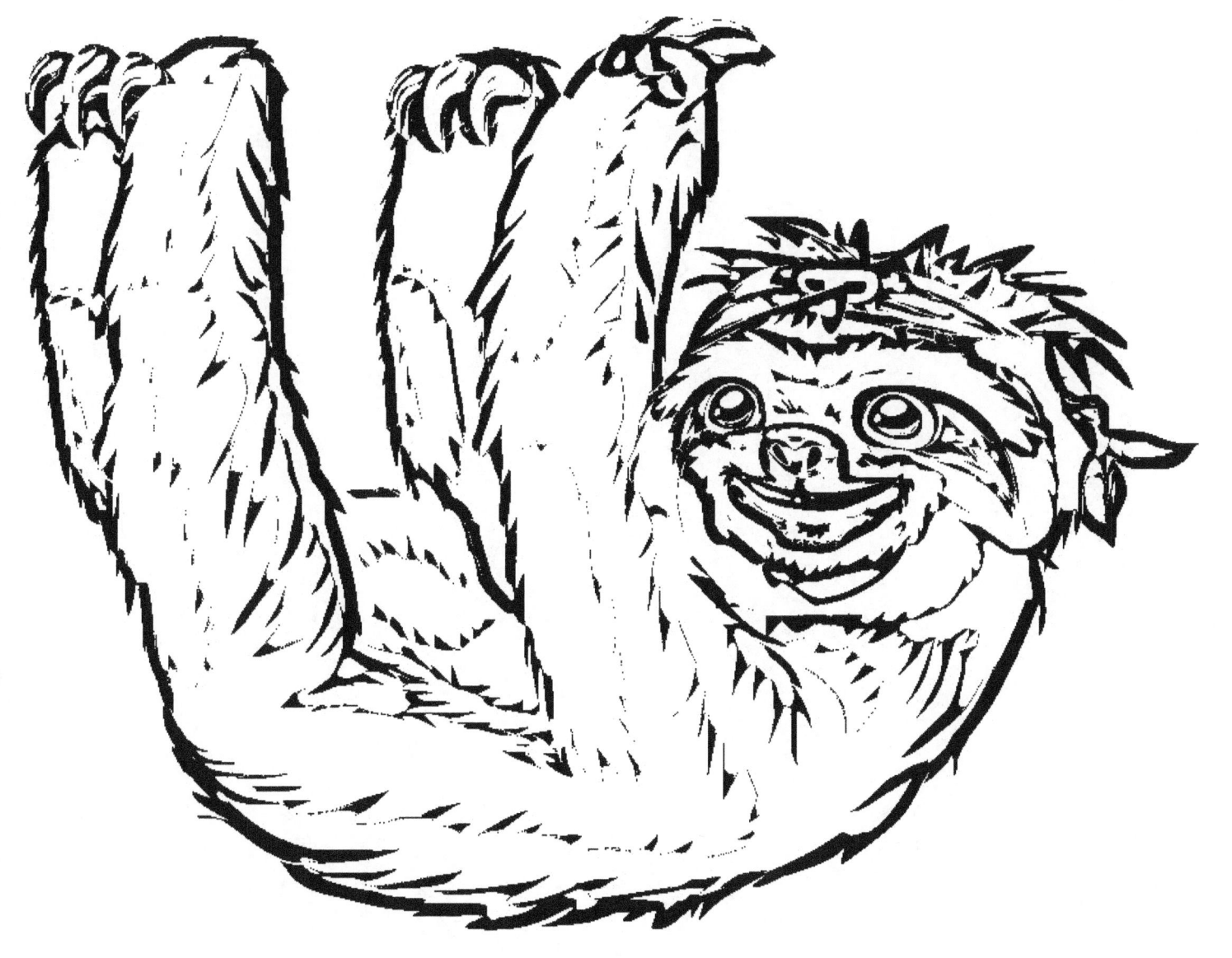

SLOTH

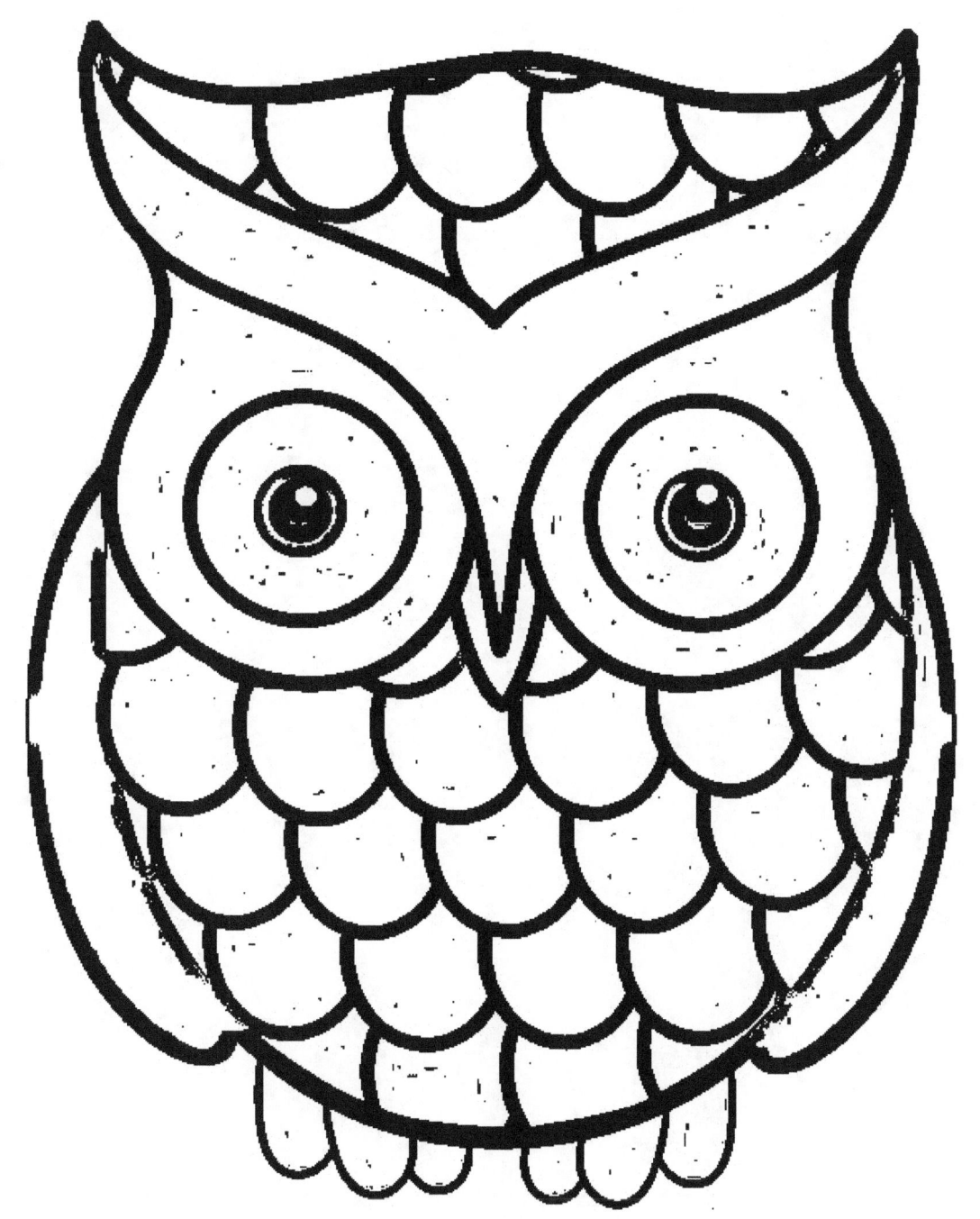

OWL

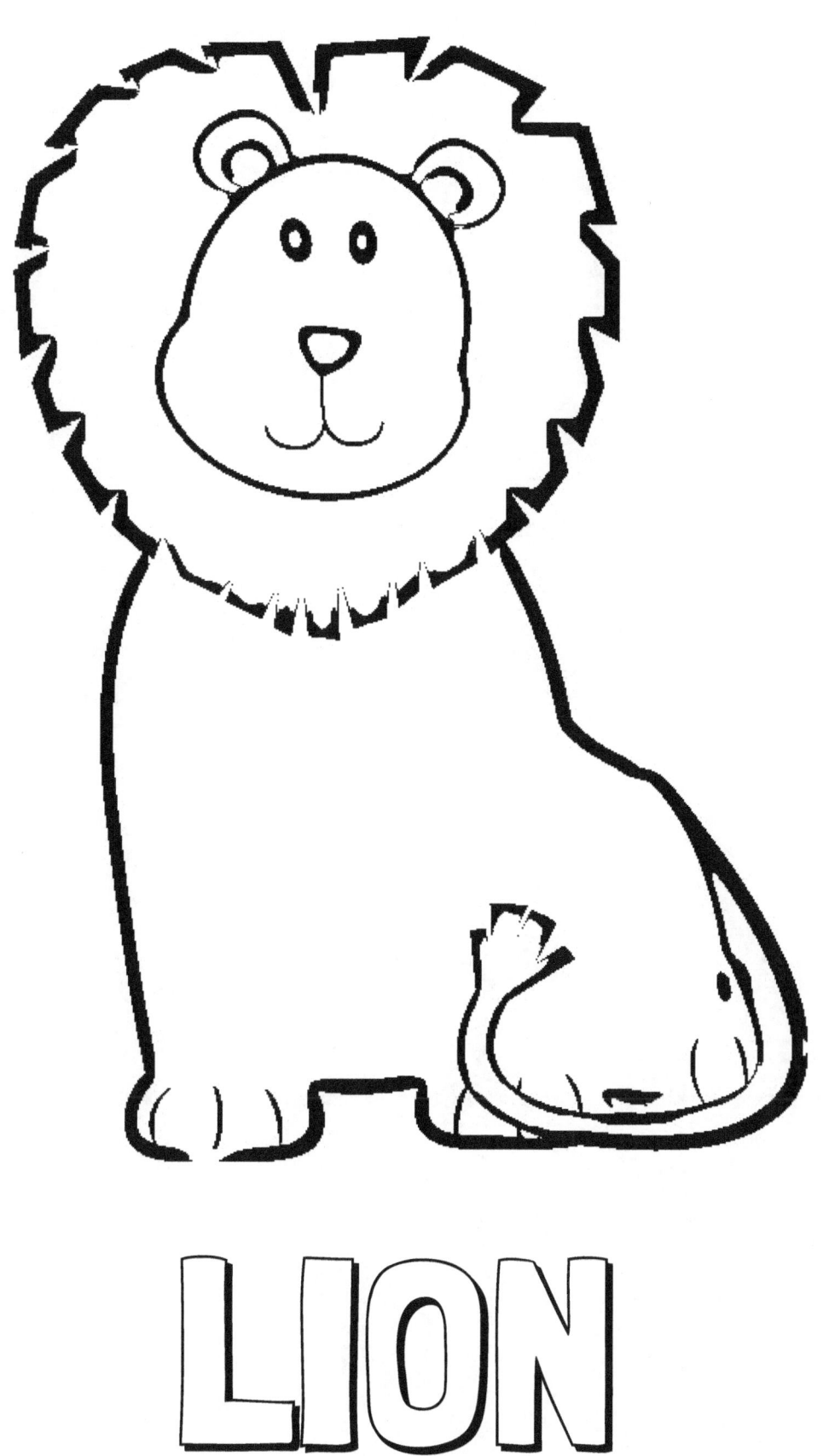

LION

www.ingramcontent.com/pod-product-compliance
Lightning Source LLC
Chambersburg PA
CBHW080643190526
45169CB00009B/3482